DINOSAURS

FUN THINGS TO LOOK FOR IN THIS BOOK

LIFT-A-FACTS

Every page has two flaps that can be lifted to reveal fun facts about the animals. One flap has a fascinating fact about a physical characteristic of the animal, and the other flap tests your knowledge about the animal with a Do You Know? question.

SIZE COMPARISONS

Look for the size icon on each page. The featured animal is compared to a 4-foot tall child.

GLOSSARY WORDS

You can learn more about the meaning of certain words by looking in the glossary located in the back of the book.

T. rex

(tie-RAN-oh-SORE-us rex)

Boom! Boom! Boom!
Who's that pounding through the forest? It's the giant Tyrannosaurus rex! This dinosaur was one of the largest that ever lived. It could gobble up to 500 pounds of meat in one bite! The T. rex wasn't picky about its food either—it would eat every bit of its prey, including bones, skin, and teeth.

The T. rex had a **huge** and **very heavy head,** but there were **holes** in it, so it could have been even **heavier.**

This dinosaur lived **closer in time** to **humans** than the first dinosaurs. The T. rex lived right before dinosaurs became **extinct.**

Inches   0   1   2   3   4   5

Centimeters   0   1   2   3   4   5   6   7   8   9   10   11   12   13

The T. rex **walked** on its **hind legs** and used its **long, HEAVY** tail for **balance**

DO YOU KNOW... what the name **Tyrannosaurus rex** means?

The largest tooth found of a T. rex is 12 inches long.

6 7 8 9 10 11 **12** 13 14 15

15 16 17 18 19 20 21 22 23 24 25 26 27 28 29 30 31 32 33 34 35 36 37 38

The velociraptor had at least one **retractable claw** on each foot. They may have used their claws to **catch** and hold their **prey.**

The velociraptor's claws were around three inches long.

inches 0 1 2 3 4 5 6 7 8 9

Centimeters 0 1 2 3 4 5 6 7 8 9 10 11 12 13 14 15 16 17 18 19 20 21 22 23

The velociraptor was **about** the **same size** as a **TURKEY.**

Velociraptor
(vel-ah-si-Rap-tor)

Is that a dinosaur covered in feathers? Yes, it's a velociraptor! In recent years, paleontologists have discovered that the velociraptor was a feathered dinosaur. Even though Velociraptor didn't fly, it had some things in common with birds—it laid eggs and probably tended to its nest like a bird.

The velociraptor was a *very* fast runner! It could run 25 miles per hour—that's about the same **speed** cars travel on some streets.

10   11   12   13   14   15

25 26 27 28 29 30 31 32 33 34 35 36 37 38

Stegosaurus

(STEG-oh-SORE-us)

Do you recognize this dinosaur with its armored plates? It's a stegosaurus! Stegosaurus was not the smartest of dinosaurs. It had a small brain, only about the size of a walnut—one of the smallest among all dinosaurs. The stegosaurus lived so long ago that it never lived to see low-lying grasses—the vegetation didn't exist yet.

It's believed that the stegosaurus had **one feature** that **not all** dinosaurs had—**cheeks.**

Stegosaurus was an **HERBIVORE.** This means it did not eat **meat** like some other dinosaurs. It ate **plants** and also small rocks to help **MASH UP** the plants in its stomach.

DO YOU KNOW...

What the name **Stegosaurus** means?

The **spiked** tail of a stegosaurus is called a **thagomizer.**

DO YOU KNOW...

how many
TEETH
Triceratops
had?

Triceratops

(try-SERRA-tops)

This dinosaur may have looked fierce with its body covered in armor and its three large pointed horns, but it did not hunt other dinosaurs—it ate only plants. It had short legs and a very heavy body so it probably didn't move very fast.

The name *Triceratops horridus* means "three-horned face."

Triceratops **wasn't** the only dinosaur of its kind. Other **"horn-faced"** dinosaurs existed, but **Triceratops** is the most **widely recognized.**

Paleontologists are still not sure what Triceratop's head frill was used for. It may have been used like a radiator to control body heat, or it may have protected the dinosaur's neck.

Spinosaurus

(spine-oh-SOR-us)

If you thought T. rex was the biggest dinosaur ever, meet Spinosaurus! This dinosaur holds the record as the largest meat-eating dinosaur of them all. Paleontologists believe this dinosaur also speared fish out of water for a meal. Spinosaurus lived during the same time period as Sarcosuchus, the "Super Croc," so these two creatures may have fought each other to catch fish.

With its **long, thin head** and relatively **short, sharp teeth,** this dinosaur looked similar to a crocodile.

The Spinosaurus's teeth were about five inches long.

Inches	0	1	2	3	4	5
Centimeters	0 1 2 3 4 5 6 7 8 9 10 11 12 13

The spinosaurus had to **adjust** its **diet** according to the **season**.

Spinosaurus mainly walked **UPRIGHT** on its **two back legs**, but it may have occasionally walked on **all fours**.

DO YOU KNOW...

what the name **Spinosaurus** means?

Brachiosaurus was so **LARGE** it had few, if any, **predators**.

Paleontologists once thought that **Brachiosaurus** spent most of its time **underwater.** They now know this is **not true.**

Brachiosaurus

(brak-ee-oh-SORE-us)

The brachiosaurus is hard to miss with its long, long neck and small head. This type of dinosaur is called a sauropod. Unlike some dinosaurs that walked on hind legs, the brachiosaurus walked on all four legs.

It is estimated that this dinosaur ate between 440 to 880 pounds of vegetation a day—that's about the same weight as some pine trees!

DO YOU KNOW...

what the name Brachiosaurus means?

Allosaurus

(al-oh-SORE-us)

Look out! It's an allosaurus! One of the first well-known dinosaurs, this meat-eating giant had very sharp claws that it may have used to catch prey. When smaller dinosaurs saw Allosaurus, they ran for their lives! This terrifying dinosaur was a frightening predator.

The allosaurus had a jaw full of **very sharp teeth,** shaped like **mini saws.** Allosaurus constantly **shed** and **grew new teeth.**

The name **Allosaurus** means **"different lizard."**

DO YOU KNOW...

what Allosaurus used to **balance?**

Some teeth measured three to four inches in length.

Inches	0	1	2	3	4	5

Centimeters	0	1	2	3	4	5	6	7	8	9	10	11	12	13

"Big Al" is the name of the most **FAMOUS** Allosaurus **skeleton,** found in **1991.**

6   7   8   9   10   11   **12**   13   14   15

15 16 17 18 19 20 21 22 23 24 25 26 27 28 29 30 31 32 33 34 35 36 37 38

Scientists think it only took about **10 YEARS** for Apatosaurus to reach its **full size.**

DO YOU KNOW...

what the name **Apatosaurus** means?

The spikes on the thumbs were up to six inches long.

Inches 0 1 2 3 4 5 6 7 8 9

Centimeters 0 1 2 3 4 5 6 7 8 9 10 11 12 13 14 15 16 17 18 19 20 21 22 23

Apatosaurus

(ah-PAT-oh-SORE-us)

The apatosaurus, once known as the brontosaurus, had a very, very long neck! This dinosaur was a sauropod—this means it had a long neck and tail, and it walked on all four legs. Paleontologists are still not sure about its posture.

The apatosaurus is thought to be one of the **largest land animals** to ever roam the **earth**. It **weighed** about the same amount as an **18-wheeler**!

The **small babies,** or **"hatchlings"** of Apatosaurus might have been **light enough** to *run* on **two feet.**

10   11   12   13   14   15

25 26 27 28 29 30 31 32 33 34 35 36 37 38

Pteranodon

(teh-RANN-oh-don)

Is it a bird? Is it a plane? No, it's a flying reptile called Pteranodon. It is not actually a dinosaur, but it did live among the dinosaurs. Even though it could fly, it did not have feathers like a bird. When Pteranodon wasn't flying, it walked around on all four legs.

Many people think modern birds are very **distant relatives** of Pteranodons, but they're **not.** Modern birds probably came from **two-legged** dinosaurs, many of which were covered in **feathers.**

Pteranodon was **not a fighter.** It could probably **FLY AWAY** from most of its enemies.

DO YOU KNOW... how many **teeth** a pteranodon had?

Pteranodons had a **crest** on their **heads,** but **no one knows** what it was used for.

Glossary

Armor: A hard, shell-like covering on a dinosaur or other animal.

Extinct: An animal that no longer exists.

Herbivore: An animal that does not eat meat.

Paleontologist: A scientist who specializes in the study of fossils and the history of life.

Predator: An animal that eats another animal for food.

Prey: An animal that is eaten by another animal for food.

Retractable: To be able to draw a claw back in.

Skull: The structure of bones that form a dinosaur's head and face.

Vegetation: A group of plants existing in a specific area.

Scientific Consultant

Jennifer Gresham
Director of Education
Zoo New England